Spelling Today

for ages 8-9

...includes words, spelling patterns and
spelling rules recommended for
Year 4 pupils.

How to use this book:

1. Look at the rules and words featured on the right-hand pages.

2. Turn over the page to look at each word on the left-hand page.

3. Cover the word with the flap, then write the word.

4. Uncover the word to check that you haven't made a mistake.

5. Write the word again for extra practice.

Double letters

double d

muddy

sudden

double l

follow

pillow

swallow

silly

double m

common

summer

swimming

mummy

double n

funny

running

dinner

tennis

penny

double p

puppy

happy

stopped

shopping

double r

carry

marry

worry

sorry

double t

rotten

letter

better

getting

written

cotton

kettle

butter

Step 1	Step 2	Step 3
Look and learn, then cover the word with the flap.	Write the word then see if it's correct.	Write the word again. Say it as you write it.
sudden		
follow		
pillow		
swimming		
summer		
dinner		
running		
stopped		
shopping		
carry		
sorry		
letter		
getting		
silly		
funny		
happy		

Homophones

Some words sound the same...

...but they mean different things and they are spelt differently.

Look: I went <u>through</u> the gate.
I <u>threw</u> the ball to Jasdeep.

Using the word-bank at the bottom, choose the correct words to fill the gaps.

George holds his pen in his _____ hand when he _____ .

I spent the _____ day mending the _____ in the wall.

Sam _____ that I had _____ shoes.

The farmer _____ a loud noise from the _____ of cows.

Mum knows _____ to put the shoes I'm going to _____ .

Did you _____ that I have _____ pets?

In the morning I climbed the _____ tree in the garden, then in the

afternoon we went to the _____ and built sandcastles.

word-bank

beech

herd   whole

right   no

beach   heard   knew

wear

hole   know   where   writes

new

Step 1	Step 2	Step 3
Look and learn, then cover the word with the flap.	Write the word then see if it's correct.	Write the word again. Say it as you write it.
throw		
threw		
through		
know		
knew		
knowledge		
known		
right		
write		
wrote		
hole		
whole		
heard		
herd		
where		
wear		

Suffixes: al, ary, ic and ly

Words ending in al, ary, ic or ly...

...are often related to other words.

Practise these sets of words:

season	
seasonal	
nation	
national	
medicine	
medical	
person	
personal	
addition	
additional	
quiet	
quietly	
most	
mostly	
quick	
quickly	

normal	
normally	
history	
historic	
angel	
angelic	
rhyme	
rhythm	
rhythmic	
traffic	
elastic	
plastic	
library	
February	
dictionary	
necessary	

Step 1	Step 2	Step 3
Look and learn, then cover the word with the flap.	Write the word then see if it's correct.	Write the word again. Say it as you write it.
February		
quietly		
medical		
season		
nation		
addition		
library		
necessary		
dictionary		
rhyme		
rhythm		
elastic		
quickly		
national		
additional		
angel		

8

Use the words from the word-bank...

...to fill the gaps in the story.

I was _____ this morning by a very loud noise. I _____ that I was

dreaming but then I _____ up properly and realised that

what I had _____ was my brother shouting. The shouting _____

then it _____ again.

"Who has been in my money box?" he shouted. "All my money has _____."

I _____ out of my bed and _____ to my bedroom door.

I _____ to _____ the handle when suddenly the door _____

and in came my brother to _____ me the empty money box.

"_____ you remember?" I _____.

"Yesterday you _____ all your money to buy football cards!"

word-bank
woken   began   asked
thought   show
heard   opened   walked   used   turn
gone   jumped   Don't   started   stopped   woke

9

Step 1	Step 2	Step 3
Look and learn, then cover the word with the flap.	Write the word then see if it's correct.	Write the word again. Say it as you write it.
woke		
woken		
think		
thought		
stopped		
started		
used		
jumped		
opened		
walked		
gone		
turn		
show		
began		
don't		
asked		

Suffixes: **ness** and **ment**

We can add the suffix **ness** to some words...

...and we can add the suffix **ment** to others.

Look: fit + ness → fitness

fair + ness →

soft + ness →

kind + ness →

cold + ness →

Look what happens when we add ness to a word which ends with a consonant then y:

Look: crazy + ness → craziness

↖ change y to an i

happy + ness →

silly + ness →

tidy + ness →

naughty + ness →

Look: move + ment → movement

manage + ment →

govern + ment →

engage + ment →

enjoy + ment →

Here are some more words to practise:

environment   ornament   document

Step 1	Step 2	Step 3
Look and learn, then cover the word with the flap.	Write the word then see if it's correct.	Write the word again. Say it as you write it.
fairness		
happiness		
silliness		
tidiness		
craziness		
kindness		
coldness		
enjoy		
enjoyment		
manage		
management		
govern		
government		
environment		
naughty		
naughtiness		

12

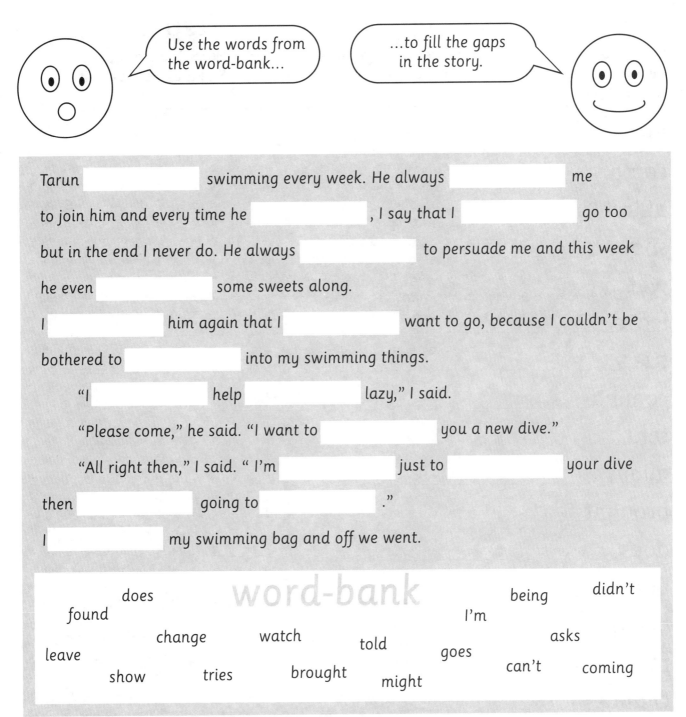

Use the words from the word-bank...

...to fill the gaps in the story.

Tarun _____ swimming every week. He always _____ me to join him and every time he _____ , I say that I _____ go too but in the end I never do. He always _____ to persuade me and this week he even _____ some sweets along.

I _____ him again that I _____ want to go, because I couldn't be bothered to _____ into my swimming things.

"I _____ help _____ lazy," I said.

"Please come," he said. "I want to _____ you a new dive."

"All right then," I said. " I'm _____ just to _____ your dive then _____ going to _____ ."

I _____ my swimming bag and off we went.

word-bank

does   being   didn't

found   I'm

change   watch   told   asks

leave

show   tries   brought   might   goes   can't   coming

13

Step 1	Step 2	Step 3
Look and learn, then cover the word with the flap.	Write the word then see if it's correct.	Write the word again. Say it as you write it.
I'm		
can't		
didn't		
show		
watch		
leave		
tries		
coming		
told		
might		
brought		
does		
goes		
being		
found		
change		

14

More suffixes

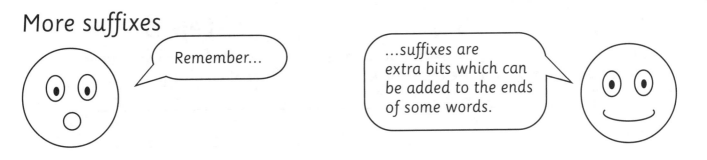

Remember...

...suffixes are extra bits which can be added to the ends of some words.

Practise these sets of words:

apology	
apologise	
short	
shorten	
strength	
strengthen	
champion	
championship	
member	
membership	
child	
childhood	
educate	
education	

dictate	
dictation	
stupid	
stupidity	
like	
likely	
likeness	
likelihood	
beauty	
beautiful	
careful	
wonderful	
painful	
awful	

Step 1	Step 2	Step 3
Look and learn, then cover the word with the flap.	Write the word then see if it's correct.	Write the word again. Say it as you write it.
apology		
apologise		
short		
shorten		
child		
childhood		
member		
membership		
educate		
education		
like		
likely		
unlikely		
beautiful		
careful		
awful		

Words which end in f

When a word ends with the letter f...

...we usually change the f to **ves** to make the word plural.

Look: half ⟶ halves

When a word ends in double f ... we just add s.

cliff ⟶ cliffs

Singular	Plural
calf ⟶	
leaf ⟶	
loaf ⟶	
scarf ⟶	
shelf ⟶	
thief ⟶	
wolf ⟶	

Singular	Plural
sniff ⟶	
puff ⟶	
cuff ⟶	
cliff ⟶	
whiff ⟶	

Practise these cases:

wife	⟶	wives
	⟶	

life	⟶	lives
	⟶	

knife	⟶	knives
	⟶	

chief	⟶	chiefs
	⟶	

Step 1 Look and learn, then cover the word with the flap.	Step 2 Write the word then see if it's correct.	Step 3 Write the word again. Say it as you write it.
half		
halves		
leaf		
leaves		
thief		
thieves		
wolf		
wolves		
wife		
wives		
knife		
knives		
life		
lives		
chief		
chiefs		

More word endings

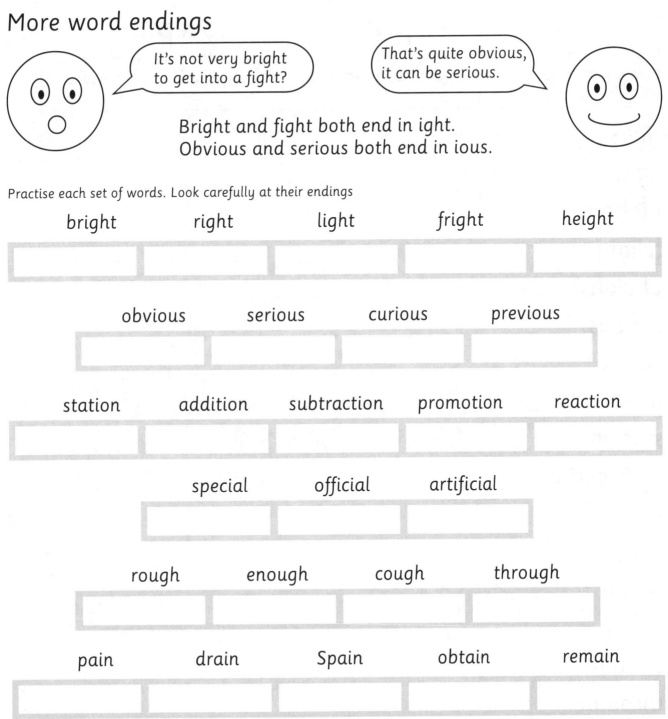

It's not very bright to get into a fight?

That's quite obvious, it can be serious.

Bright and fight both end in ight.
Obvious and serious both end in ious.

Practise each set of words. Look carefully at their endings

bright   right   light   fright   height

obvious   serious   curious   previous

station   addition   subtraction   promotion   reaction

special   official   artificial

rough   enough   cough   through

pain   drain   Spain   obtain   remain

Step 1	Step 2	Step 3
Look and learn, then cover the word with the flap.	Write the word then see if it's correct.	Write the word again. Say it as you write it.
right		
light		
night		
height		
obvious		
serious		
curious		
drain		
station		
subtraction		
special		
Spain		
rough		
cough		
enough		
through		

Some prefixes

Prefixes go at the start of some words.

Look at the sets of words below. Then find the right ones to fit the gaps in the sentences.

ad words	advise adjective advent adverb adventure advance admire adjust

I [   ] you for going on such a brave [   ] .

An [   ] describes a noun and an [   ] tells us how

something is done.

al words	also alone always already almost Although altogether along

I [   ] go shopping on Saturday.

I sometimes go [   ] and sometimes with my friends.

There are six of us [   ] . [   ] we all get on well, I do have

one best friend. We get [   ] really well.

Note: **all right** should always be written in two words.

Step 1	Step 2	Step 3
Look and learn, then cover the word with the flap.	Write the word then see if it's correct.	Write the word again. Say it as you write it.
all right		
also		
altogether		
adjective		
advent		
adjust		
along		
always		
advance		
adverb		
almost		
although		
adventure		
advise		
already		
admire		

As soon as I got up this _____ I had to rush out to play football.

It's not very _____ that I go anywhere without _____ breakfast

but I don't need _____ to eat so I just had a _____ of crisps

_____ I walked along.

The _____ half of the match went quite badly but we played much

_____ in the _____ half. I've _____ scored a goal in a

proper match _____ but _____ was my big day.

At the start of the second _____ the score was _____ nil-nil.

_____ the ball shot in my direction. I stopped it with my left foot, then spun

_____ and shot with my right. Goal!

---

word-bank

half   second   much

morning   today

better   packet   while   before   often   around

never   Suddenly   first   any   still

23

Step 1	Step 2	Step 3
Look and learn, then cover the word with the flap.	Write the word then see if it's correct.	Write the word again. Say it as you write it.
much		
any		
while		
today		
first		
second		
half		
before		
still		
better		
packet		
suddenly		
morning		
never		
around		
often		

Useful words

We've written some sets of words.

Choose the correct words to fill each gap in the sentences.

above below	Moles live _____ the ground. Squirrels live _____ the ground.
every number year	The _____ of people in the world gets bigger _____ _____ .
sometimes during	There are _____ heavy storms _____ the summer.
asleep awake usually	When I go to bed I try to stay _____ for as long as possible but I _____ fall _____ quite quickly.
only young upon until inside near high place	Once _____ a time there was a beautiful, _____ princess. She lived _____ a very _____ tower. Her _____ company was a tiny mouse _____ she was found by a handsome prince. He had searched _____ and far before he had reached the _____ where she lived.

Step 1	Step 2	Step 3
Look and learn, then cover the word with the flap.	Write the word then see if it's correct.	Write the word again. Say it as you write it.
during		
above		
below		
inside		
high		
year		
near		
number		
every		
asleep		
awake		
usually		
young		
place		
sometimes		
until		

Common letter strings

Some groups of letters often appear together.

Can you give me some examples?

Examples: **ive** appears in:
ear appears in:

live massive give expensive
hear heard wear learn

ive

live
alive
massive
give
expensive

ear

hear
heard
appears
wear
learn

our

pour
hour
favour
favourite

wa

want
watch
water
wait

wo

woman
women
won't
would
two

au

because
sausage
autumn
haul

Step 1	Step 2	Step 3
Look and learn, then cover the word with the flap.	Write the word then see if it's correct.	Write the word again. Say it as you write it.
live		
alive		
expensive		
hear		
heard		
appears		
wear		
watch		
water		
wait		
woman		
women		
two		
because		
favourite		
autumn		

Common letter strings

You find i and e together in words like pie and friend, but also when you take a y off some words.

For example when cry becomes cries.

Practise the words in these sets:

ie

cries

tries

babies

ponies

piece

pie

stories

friend

ry

hairy

story

February

library

ck

stick

pickle

trickle

ou

out

shout

outside

without

our

hour

round

found

could

should

would

oo

look

book

cook

broom

gloomy

Step 1	Step 2	Step 3
Look and learn, then cover the word with the flap.	Write the word then see if it's correct.	Write the word again. Say it as you write it.
cries		
ladies		
piece		
story		
stories		
trickle		
outside		
without		
library		
libraries		
hour		
could		
should		
reply		
replies		
replied		

Double s

Words have been missed out of the passage below.

Some of the words have a double s. You can find all the words in the word-banks.

word-bank

possible   such   guess   miss   thought   lesson   other   first

In our _____ _____ yesterday morning we had a spelling test. I _____ it was quite easy but I did have to _____ some words and I also had to _____ one word out because it was _____ a difficult one. It's _____ that I got all of the _____ words right.

word-bank

between   success   different   together   pass   across   under   less   both

If you get _____ than half marks in the test, you don't _____ and you have to do it again. That happened to me once and my best friend got _____ half marks as well. We practised _____ for the repeat test but she had _____ mistakes to me. After the second test we had to pass the papers _____ the desks to be marked. They were shared _____ different people. I had much more _____ this time. We _____ were very pleased.

31

Step 1 Look and learn, then cover the word with the flap.	Step 2 Write the word then see if it's correct.	Step 3 Write the word again. Say it as you write it.
guess		
lesson		
success		
together		
both		
under		
between		
across		
different		
less		
pass		
possible		
such		
thought		
other		
miss		

Common letter strings

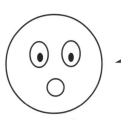

A nice policeman put some spice in his rice...

...and fed some mice twice.

There are lots if **ice** words in the speech bubbles.

Practise the words in these sets:

ice

mice	
spice	
police	
twice	

ough

tough	
enough	
rough	
though	
through	
thought	
thorough	

sc

science	
scent	
fascinating	

gh

laugh	
sigh	
high	
thigh	

ch

chair	
church	
charity	
such	

ow

brown	
now	
how	
glow	
follow	
following	
know	

Step 1	Step 2	Step 3
Look and learn, then cover the word with the flap.	Write the word then see if it's correct.	Write the word again. Say it as you write it.
following		
laugh		
police		
twice		
though		
through		
thought		
thorough		
science		
chair		
know		
known		
sigh		
high		
flow		
follow		

34

More letter strings

Practise each set of words.

Look carefully at the strings of letters.

ist

artist
finalist
violinist
pianist
artistic

ible

horrible
terrible
possible
impossible

able

miserable
probable

Look how it changes

probably

sion

decision
explosion
television
division

tion

addition
subtraction
multiplication

Look at these pairs of words:

minimum
minibus

majorette
usherette

duckling
gosling

microscope
microphone

35

Step 1	Step 2	Step 3
Look and learn, then cover the word with the flap.	Write the word then see if it's correct.	Write the word again. Say it as you write it.
artistic		
horrible		
terrible		
impossible		
miserable		
probably		
addition		
subtraction		
multiplication		
division		
television		
explosion		
minimum		
duckling		
microscope		
microphone		